I0881213

the
LATE SEASON

the LATE SEASON

patti sinclair

AT BAY press

WINNIPEG

The Late Season

Design and layout by Lucas c Pauls and M. C. Joudrey.

Published by At Bay Press February 2025.

Library and Archives Canada cataloguing in publication is available upon request.

ISBN 978-1-998779-58-1

Printed and bound in Canada.

This book is printed on acid free paper that is 100% recycled ancient forest friendly (100% post-consumer recycled).

FSC www.fsc.org MIX Paper | Supporting responsible forestry FSC® C016245

First Edition

10 9 8 7 6 5 4 3 2 1

atbaypress.com

Canada Council for the Arts / Conseil des arts du Canada

We acknowledge the support of the Canada Council for the Arts.

Manitoba Arts Council / Conseil des arts du Manitoba

With the generous support of the Manitoba Arts Council.

For Dad, Michael, & Steph

how the angle of the sun silvers
the black screen of the porch
mother-cat made larger by the late-day
August shadow
sniffs for volunteer crumbs

with this light the whole world alters

the sink, after much rustling of gritty
silverware
drains, gurgles, and the newly crossed-
over teenager
bounds upstairs
does this serpentine thing with her
head
like she is painting an *S* from the
bottom up
while two white moths flit over the
lawn
        let feral in the spring
their wings hover, deciding on which
head
of wild carrot
they will rest

2

•

The LATE SEASON

patti sinclair

the sun sits low
phone rings early
she is called to sort low-bush ii
blueberries
she has slept beside me; stomachache
at midnight
crows absent at daybreak
newly cool in the bedroom,
unidentified
bites on hip and thigh itch

don't yet know why

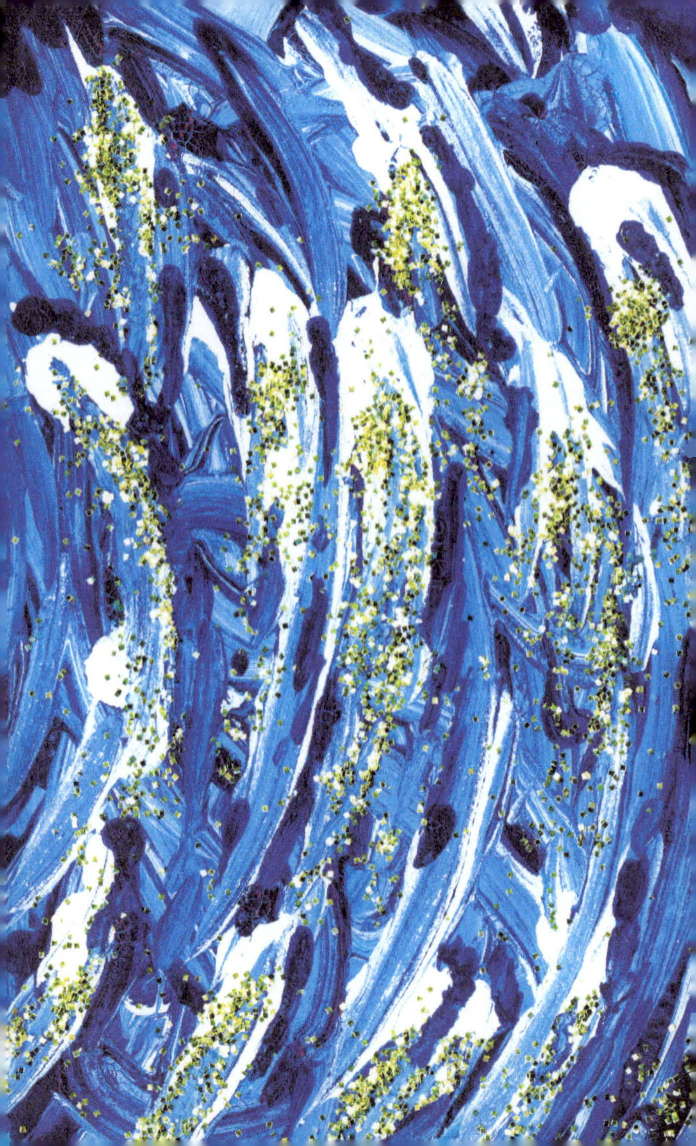

towels on the line, post-tropical-Daniel
which gives only rain
can't see the sun, but the air a
welcoming warmth
contrasted by the first day of wearing a
sweater
inside

a dream about aunt, uncle, and cousin
visiting
both Aunt and Uncle deceased in
recent times
am surprised they look so young,
vibrant

your chair empty, when they enter the
living room

windswept day
sheets dry despite the unseen sun

6

•

The LATE SEASON

patti sinclair

family meeting about kittens
'Roguie McRogue' has caught on to
the one named after you

you, gone now

discuss how we may find homes for
the rest
posters at the post office, vet's
'Free Kittens' sign at Saturday market
maybe to the small pet shop

8

•

The LATE SEASON

patti sinclair

concerns about a cranky friend
she is nervous about the start of classes
this blueberry cleaner
going on to her fourth day of late
summer employment

    where has the summer gone?

desirous of something from the past
cannot name, cannot have

10

•

The LATE SEASON

patti sinclair

I walk down the lane to the Grand
Atlantic
Dip your feet. Walk with me. I will
hold you always.
I walk, the water warm
Walk with me.
the bottom soft with few ocean
pebbles
walk to the line between water and
shore
    seaweed bleached
step over it, sit on sandstone rock
find ocean droplets on my hand
    or could they be tears?
taste is the same

the best-swimmer-movie-star from the
fifties
you would know her name

it keeps slipping from my tongue

12

•

The LATE SEASON

patti sinclair

vii

she sits in black, hood over her crown
book about anchors rests under my
elbow
archway of vines outside the window
hear an unseen child's cry of delight,
wonder
had sunshine for days; today a mix
I wonder
      where I belong

your hometown name and sister's
tattooed on your upper arms
on banners, I can't remember
if they were inked on anchors or
shields
      embarrassed, you hid them

14

The LATE SEASON

patti sinclair

viii

sun in my eyes, see the rainbow in my
lashes
sore lower back under
duvet cover with erratic pastel spirals
ripped and patched in various places

returned rattle of the school bus down
the road
the galloping below of sixteen kitten
paws
and the heels of her, making turkey,
marble cheese
fresh whole wheat sandwiches for
school

in this quiet of the country I hear
everything

eyes looking, wondering
if it is all
      enough

no more sounds downstairs
they must be gone

18

•

The LATE SEASON

patti sinclair

leaves and sun through the window
pane
play Morse code on my pillow
complete silence, but for the scratch of
this pen
still four — nine-week-old kittens in
various stages of slumber
I give into the stillness
not moving
our fourth fall here
Fall Here! Fall Here! the house
whispers

five apple trees in back with thick
heads
beaded with redding and tart beauties
arms heavy, not yet falling
      and the one newly discovered
plum tree, perfect
deep purple dusted
      white

I say a little prayer for you. Forever.

I want to send you apples.

22

•

The LATE SEASON

patti sinclair

X

I roam the house
wash dishtowels
pin them on the line
shake the trees for plums, apples
bark at the scattered litter
of three remaining kits and two adult
cats
blankets left unfolded
desk, chair, floor ripe
with paraphernalia of a few days
of living

24

•

The LATE SEASON

patti sinclair

this September sun is sweet
I bath in it, am warmed by it
        and the apple trees
wish I hadn't left the deep-dish Terra-
cotta pie plate
when we moved

just when I think I am bored or lonely
sit with it long enough
find its rhythm and grace
my unrest dissolves
and I am in want of nothing
but the sound of the banjo on the
radio
the sun silhouetting my pen tip
my posed and pressing fingers
heart beating full
of these simple, beautiful things

26

•

The LATE SEASON

patti sinclair

the sun peeks through a crater in the
clouds
most of the sky is whitewash
wakes me up to an uncrowded day
still wonder about life; my place in it
now that you are gone
    the shields you held for me

xii

28

•

The LATE SEASON

patti sinclair

the sun sits lower and the time is later
it illuminates the dust of this late
season
why do we have dust?
why must we constantly clean?

we're all dust, Honey

xiii

30

•

The LATE SEASON

patti sinclair

the sun makes shadow mountains on
this lumpy duvet
tuxedo cat, 'Roguie McRogue' tumbles
atop it
fur gleams in the sunlight
    the sheen of innocence
like brand new, black patent-leather
shoes for the first day of school

this wandering kitten
is the last to go, find a home

    and after, and again she sobs
the last of these six kitten
departures

32

•

The LATE SEASON

patti sinclair

you blew us kisses

this final image hovers
perhaps your message to me now

your last gesture

on my walk, between light and dark
I ask of The Grand Atlantic

be as graceful as you can be
    that is good enough
walk the shores
let the wind blow your hair
know it will never blow
this way again

but I don't want to drown in this biting
fierce sorrow

yet
each season we turn our gardens over,
say
good-bye to the magnolia, put
warm sweaters on-

but I miss him

Yes

miss him well

36

•

The LATE SEASON

patti sinclair

when you decided it was time to sail

saw you hover
negotiate with both sides
      seek out
the schedule
in the comfort of pale light
in your last room
by the window

patti sinclair gratefully creates on the land of the People of the Papaschase First Nation. Author of one memoir and five poetry chapbooks, most recently, *The Rightful Skin,* with Rose Garden Press, a featured poem, 'The Brine', forthcoming with Capital City Press and poetry in *We'Moon: The Growing Edge,* patti's poetry attempts to ground fierce and beautiful impulses found in private moments and collective rituals. She relishes sharing her works out-loud, having performed in poetry, music, and art festivals.

OUR AT BAY PRESS
ARTISTIC COMMUNITY:

Publisher – **Matt Joudrey**
Managing Editor – **Alana Brooker**
Substantive Editor – **Chelene Knight**
Copy and Proof Editor – **Courtney Bill**
Graphic Designer – **Lucas c Pauls**
Layout – **Lucas c Pauls** and **Matt Joudrey**
Publicity and Marketing – **Savita Singh**

Thanks for purchasing this book and
for supporting authors and artists.
As a token of gratitude, please scan the
QR code for exclusive content from this title.